i

A POST MODERN APPROACH TO U.S. POLICY IN THE ARCTIC

On 16 January 2012, a Russian oil tanker delivered 1.3 million gallons of oil products to the frozen and fuel deprived residents of Nome, Alaska. A United States Coast Guard Icebreaker cut a path for the tanker through the last 300 miles of sea ice to ensure the successful transfer of supplies. The rescue mission, the first ever to supply fuel during the winter months, was necessary due to early and abnormally large storms last fall in the Arctic.[1] Joint, civil-military, and multi-nation actions like this demonstrate the collaboration and cooperation necessary for successful operations above the Arctic Circle.

The nexus of post modern state interaction, the employment of military force, and climate change pose a tremendous challenge for our political leaders and strategists in the next decade and the most likely location is in the Arctic. The increased interdependence of nations caused by globalization, the continuing trend away from state on state warfare, and the problems associated with increased access to the Arctic create an opportunity for the United States to take the lead in improving international cooperation and promoting greater interdependence among nation states. Instead of individual nations "colonizing" and defending their own territory above the Arctic Circle where the cost, the unforgiving environment, and the receding ice influence a nation's decisions, it seems more logical that those nations with claims in the region work together in order to profit from their efforts, protect their interests, and police the area.

This paper will analyze the post cold war international system, including changes to the use of military force, and climate change; discuss how those changes impact the Arctic region, America, and other international actors; and make recommendations for modifying the strategic policy of the United States. As the recent rescue mission in Alaska shows, multilateral cooperation in the Arctic is required and necessary due to the extreme climate, the abundance of vital resources, territorial claims, and the potential for military conflict.

Climate Change

The ice covering the Arctic region is now almost half of what it was a half century ago due to changes in the Earth's climate.[2] The annual average temperature for the Arctic has increased almost two degrees Fahrenheit against the thirty year average from 1961 to 1990 and the winter seasonal temperature is now nine degrees higher than it was during the Kennedy Administration.[3] These changes not only make summer passage through the north a possibility by 2030, but increase opportunities for resource exploitation throughout the area and threaten the way of life for wildlife and native peoples.

There is potential for the Arctic to serve as a conduit for limited shipping between Asia and Europe in the next few years. The melting of the ice sheets in the summer will open the Northwest and Northeast Passages reducing both transit time and the cost of shipments. Estimates indicate a savings of as many as ten days and as much as $300,000 dollars per ship are possible.[4] Another significant benefit of a northern route is avoiding pirates operating in the other choke points around the world, but the Arctic sea ice will continue to deny passage most of the year and ships would require special hulls and other expensive support requirements to operate there.

The Arctic region also holds almost 30 percent of the world's undiscovered resources, including almost 15 percent of the oil and over 30 percent of the remaining natural gas.[5] Additionally, the largest zinc and palladium mines as well as one of the largest copper mines in the world are north of the Arctic Circle.[6] In the past, these areas were not economically or geographically viable or affordable to exploit, but soon they will be completely accessible to the countries that lay claim to the territory. While these resources may not be critical to the overall economies of Canada, Denmark, Norway, and the United States, extractions from the Arctic provide leverage against nations like Russia, China, and India who require the materials to continue to grow their economies.[7]

International treaties protect Antarctica from confrontation and exploitation.[8] Unfortunately, the Arctic was not afforded the same status by the United Nations and the impact on the region due to interest in developing the Arctic's resources is disturbing. Retreating ice threatens the livelihood of the indigenous people, the habitats of many animals, and creates friction as sovereignty issues quickly elevate from boundary concerns to altercations involving strategic interests. While new fishing areas and precious materials increase the quality of life for many people around the world, pollution from cruise ships taking advantage of new routes into the region threaten the homes of native North Americans, jeopardize the purity of Arctic ecosystems, and potentially force the relocation of polar bears, harp seals, and the Arctic Fox. Fortunately, the likelihood of states going to war with one another over these types of issues is low, but future economic benefits to the Arctic nations threaten to increase tension in the area.

Extreme weather changes in the Arctic already influence normal protocols followed by state actors. As the successful mission in Nome, Alaska, earlier this year illustrates, cooperation and common purpose are possible and necessary in remote and inhospitable areas. Serious damage to the Arctic is possible if stakeholders fail to plan and resource for the obvious changes coming in the next decade. Not only is environmental and personal tragedy likely to occur in the region, but the potential for confrontation between the countries operating in the Arctic increases exponentially.

Military Force

Force is the essence of military action, whether tank army versus tank army or infantryman versus infantryman, and remains virtually unchanged since the first battle occurred. While strategy differs, Sun Tzu favored an indirect approach and Jomini operating on interior lines, the utility of force has never been questioned. However, recently the employment of force, relatively static since Napoleon assembled his armies to conquer Europe, has changed.[9] As the nations operating in the Arctic begin to assess their force requirements and employment criteria, these changes influence their planning.

Countries and their political leaders continue to rely on their militaries to advance and protect their interests. But armies no longer require large expanses of territory to fight. Today, engagements can occur anywhere, at anytime, between regular and irregular forces. The countries with the strongest, best equipped, and most technologically advanced military force often fail to achieve their desired endstate.[10]

The main reason for disconnects between the ends and the means is a lack of understanding on the part of strategic leaders who deploy forces without recognizing the capabilities of their militaries. Difficulties primarily occur when forces deploy on non-standard missions where the armies have not been properly trained and equipped to

4

execute effectively. As Operation Iraqi Freedom showed, the United States military performed well during the initial force on force campaign culminating with the capitulation of Saddam Hussein. They had practiced and honed their battle drills during years of mock battles at the National Training Center and Joint Readiness Training Center. However, when the war transitioned to Phase IV, a mission set rarely thought about or prepared for, the United States military quickly became overwhelmed.[11] Sir Rupert Smith further argues that in the formation of forces "money has been the greatest deciding factor in the structure of a force."[12] Not only does cost impact the size and shape of the current force but it has a limiting effect on the future force as well. Unless a country requires a large force for survival, like North Korea or Israel, it is unlikely that resources will be available to maintain them in the future.[13]

In order to get beyond financial constraints when utilizing force in the future, Smith offers five elements for leaders to use to help them assess any situation requiring military force:

Forming – what type of force structure is required to accomplish the mission

Deploying – how to move and where to locate the force required

Directing – who will lead and employ the force to accomplish the mission

Sustaining – how will the force be resourced and supplied

Recovering – how will responsibilities be transferred amongst the force[14]

When applied to the Arctic, the challenge becomes particularly difficult. Ideally, nations operating in the region recognize the complexity of the situation and understand that working alone is not feasible. But coalitions are not easy either; when functioning as part of a multi-nation force, national caveats can preclude action or require separate and distinct missions.[15]

Each Arctic nation has national interests to protect and attempts to influence the region for its own benefit. The primary method of influence is the deployment and employment of military force. However, each nation with interests in the Arctic has its own strengths and weaknesses and no single nation is capable of dominating the entire spectrum of operations because the cost in manpower, equipment, technology, and dollars is prohibitive. The challenge for all of them is to maximize their influence and gain access to the most resources while at the same time reducing their own cost and risk. As observed with the Russian and American operation in Nome, Alaska, the successful execution of specific missions in the Arctic by a multi-nation force is possible. The question is whether or not nation states are ready to move toward a universal application of this type of interaction.

Post Modern World

The end of the Cold War brought to conclusion a physical struggle between East and West, and between ideas. Nations had operated for almost 350 years on the principles of imperialism, colonial empire, and a balance of power. However, with the breakup of the Soviet Union responsibility shifted back to individual nations that were unprepared to participate in an international system. The result was a new paradigm characterized by pre-modern, modern, and post modern states. These changes directly impact the way that Arctic nations interrelate and cooperate with one another.

According to British diplomat, author, and advisor to former Prime Minister Tony Blair, Robert Cooper, we now live in a divided world.[16] Pre-modern states are weak, failing, and most often authoritarian. Their economies are usually agrarian and religion serves as the intellectual basis of understanding. In the realm of foreign affairs a pre-modern nation's relationships with others are chaotic.[17] Afghanistan best exemplifies the pre-modern state. The Afghan central government controls only the ground it physically occupies with its security forces. It is unable to govern due to ineffective institutions, and its democracy will remain dependent upon foreign handouts for the foreseeable future. To successfully develop the Arctic, political and economic stakeholders must establish strong working relationships with the mostly pre-modern population. The limited infrastructure, harsh environment, and hierarchical nature of the native communities require governments and corporations to focus on accommodation rather than confrontation. While the Arctic is not a failing state like Afghanistan, reluctance to incorporate the indigenous people of the region into the overall solution poses a risk to any coalition or cooperative venture.

Modern states portray the characteristics of the classical state system. They retain significant military forces and are prepared to use them against one another. In order to achieve their strategic endstates their government institutions are more organized, bureaucratic, and centralized than those in pre-modern states.[18] As a modern nation takes on greater responsibility for the health, education, and welfare of its citizens, the economy begins to shift from an agrarian focus to a more commercial and industrial one and interstate relations move to the forefront and nationalistic passions begin to drive both domestic and foreign policy.[19]

Of the five Arctic nations, Russia appears the most reliant on its military and the most likely to use force if its interests are threatened. Moscow believes the Arctic is a fundamental part of its national identity and critical to its resurgence.[20] Ideally, the United States, Canada, Denmark, Norway, and Russia will work together and through international institutions to avoid confrontation and settle disputes. Similar to the way Norway and Russia agreed to split and share 175,000 square kilometers of the Barents Sea in September 2010.[21] Clearly, the benefits of collaboration are greater than the risk of war. The challenge is convincing Russia that sharing both the responsibility and the rewards of the Arctic protects its vital interests.

Post modern states have adopted economic and institutional methods that allow power to be diffused in order to take advantage of the global environment.[22] National interests become more and more transparent and their successful achievement is increasingly dependent on other state and non-state actors. As Cooper states, "the post modern system does not rely on balance; nor does it emphasize sovereignty…," it relies upon transparency, mutual openness, interdependence, and mutual vulnerability.[23] The majority of the Arctic nations fall into this category. Capitalizing on this type of behavior allows the Arctic nations to maintain security and exploit the region's resources for the benefit of the international community without causing a military confrontation.

The optimal solution is the establishment of formal treaties and agreements between the Arctic nations. The irrelevance of borders in the Arctic and the recognition that one nation's success is directly tied to the success of another nation due to the harsh environment naturally drives interdependency among the nations. Ultimately, it is by unselfishly limiting one's use of force in order to solve a problem that builds cooperation for the greater good of civilization. The Arctic is the perfect laboratory for this type of experiment.

Arctic Interests

The United States, Canada, Denmark, Norway, and Russia all assert some level of sovereignty in the Arctic. Climate change impacts each nation due to its influence on resource availability, access, and security. In addition, the capabilities of their militaries and relationships with one another drive each country's individual goals and the future of regional cooperation and interdependence.

Canada. The Canadian Arctic is a large maritime area that shares its borders with several nations. Canadian politicians and journalists describe it as "an integral part of [their] national identity."[24] However, current disagreements with the United States, Denmark, and Russia impact both freedom of navigation and claims to the continental shelf. Failure to resolve these issues limits investment, resource extraction, and economic gain. Legal challenges in the Beaufort Sea threaten a natural gas pipeline that could deliver more than 1.2 billion cubic feet of gas per day.[25] As access through the Northwest Passage improves, vulnerabilities increase across the entirety of Canadian borders. Not only will commercial traffic in the region grow, but tourism and illegal movements will increase as well.[26] In order to monitor the threat and protect its national interests, Canada must invest in security and "exercise control over and defend Canada's sovereignty in the Arctic."[27]

The cost to improve Canada's defenses is significant. New ice breaking ships run close to a billion dollars each, improvements to naval port facilities will cost well over $100 million dollars, and additional patrol aircraft will add another half a billion dollars to an already shrinking military budget.[28] Canada also wants to increase its permanent military presence in the Arctic. While it currently conducts joint military exercises with the United States and Danish navies, it is also expanding its diplomatic efforts to resolve territorial issues with Russia to reduce any potential military tension.

Canada's relationship with the United States remains strong both militarily and diplomatically due to its common border and shared values. Continued military cooperation in the Arctic stabilizes the region, while increasing diplomatic efforts reduces territorial concerns between the two nations. By continuing a dual track approach in the future, Canada and the United States increase opportunities for collective and cooperative action with each other and the other regional actors.

Denmark. Greenland, controlled by the Danish Government for almost 300 years, is the reason for Denmark's claim to the Arctic. Greenland received "home rule" status in 1979 and "self rule" in 2009 allowing residents a greater share of revenues from national resources. However, Denmark is unlikely to grant Greenland its independence and still retains responsibility for its foreign and security affairs.[29]

The Danes are very forceful regarding exploration and establishing their claims in the Arctic. It appears to be their intent to document their sovereignty through scientific data collection and utilize existing international law to protect their interests. However, similar to Canada, difficulties with boundaries and borders have the potential to limit the extraction of trillions of cubic feet of natural gas and billions of barrels of oil.[30] Utilization of international principles and existing treaties is clearly the best way for Denmark, Canada, and Norway to ensure their access to resources and to avoid confrontation.

Militarily, Danish Armed Forces continue to increase the frequency of their activities in the Arctic. They recently spent upwards of $200 million dollars to upgrade their ability to operate in the region and seek closer military cooperation with the United States, Canada, and Russia.[31] Like Canada and Norway, Denmark will continue to slowly build their military capacity in the Arctic and take advantage of cooperative military partnerships to hedge against unsuccessful diplomatic efforts. However, in the near future, expect Denmark's main effort to focus on cooperation and diplomacy as they attempt to take advantage of their Presidency in the Arctic Council.

Norway. The Norwegian Government is influenced by two significant factors with regard to its Arctic policies. The first is the region's economic potential as it pertains to oil, gas, and fishing. The second is its common border and long standing relationship with Russia.

Today, the oil and gas industry alone is responsible for 22% of Norway's GDP.[32] As the ice melts in the Arctic, expect Norway to position itself to take advantage of new and greater opportunities. Increased maritime traffic and commercial fisheries requires the advancement of policies that conform to international law and are in line with very strict environmentally friendly domestic legislation.

Since the earliest days of the Cold War, Norway has been engaged with Russia due to its shared border. Now security concerns, climate change and other Arctic issues ensure this relationship will remain proactive, pragmatic, and cooperative.[33] As such, while diplomats look for common ground economically and environmentally, the military repositioned forces above the Arctic Circle to protect and maintain their sovereignty in the region.[34] Expect Oslo to maintain good relations with Moscow as

11

they both move forward, but Norwegian desires to preserve their national interests in the High North will simultaneously drive the improvement of their military capabilities.

Russia. Due to the size of the Russian Arctic, over 4000 miles from east to west, and the type and amount of exploitable resources, Russia is the most aggressive and militarily focused player in the region. In 2009, the government published its National Security Strategy which stated that the Polar region is Russia's top strategic resource base.[35] With Russian strength tied to its economic wealth and ability to influence markets, Arctic nations must consider Russian reaction regardless of the issue.

While the other members of the Arctic club lead with diplomacy, Russia's efforts begin with a strong military presence. Already possessing the world's largest icebreaking fleet, the Russians have begun strengthening their Border Guard Force, modernizing military equipment, and conducting training exercises and patrols in the region at levels not experienced since the Cold War.[36] Convincing the Russians to collaborate and work in a collective security environment requires patience and a willingness to ensure that their national interests are secure.

Russia's deployment of military force to protect its national interest compliments their use of international institutions to support its territorial claims. In order to accomplish its goals, Russia established as a top priority the completion of geological studies to support its claims to the outer most limits of its continental shelf. Similar to Canada in the Northwest, Russia believes that it must monitor and protect itself from threats along the Northeast Passage. As a potential high speed route between Europe and Asia, control of this movement corridor has significant strategic and economic implications if dominated by Moscow.[37] Regardless of the issue, expect Russia to position itself both militarily and diplomatically to ensure an outcome that supports its vital interests. The only unanswered question about Russia's future at this point is what the United States will do with regard to the Arctic.

U.S. Involvement

One of the greatest challenges to American involvement in the Arctic is the absence of the United States Senate's ratification of the United Nations Convention on Law of the Sea (UNCLOS). The primary purpose of this international agreement was to establish protocols for areas of the ocean that are outside national jurisdictions. As the Arctic ice melts, the importance of Article 76 of the convention increases in importance to the United States and the four other Arctic nations. Specifically, provisions of the agreement allow for nations to extend their sovereign territory from 12 miles offshore to over 200 miles.[38] As a non-party to UNCLOS, the United States cannot submit a claim to extend its currently recognized boundaries, resulting in the potential loss of trillions of dollars from additional resource exploitation.

Both the Obama and the Bush Administrations recognized the political and economic importance of the Arctic to the United States and provided strategic guidance on the subject. In January 2009, the White House released National Security Presidential Directive 66 which established the policy of the United States in order to "meet national security and homeland security needs relevant to the Arctic region"[39] and "strengthen institutions for cooperation"[40] between the Arctic nations. Additionally, the release of the 2011 Unified Command Plan reiterated the importance of the region and directed US Northern Command (NORTHCOM) to take responsibility for the area.

In May 2011, the United States made its first serious attempt to increase its diplomatic effort in the Arctic. Secretary of State Clinton's participation in ministerial level meetings of the Arctic Council was the first time an American of that rank or stature acknowledged or attended a Council function.[41] If the United States intends to establish itself as a leader in the Arctic region, then it must continue to participate in, lend its legitimacy to, and foster the growth of collective and cooperative organizations. Improving diplomatic reputations is just one of the methods to ensuring vital interests are recognized and protected.

Another way to ensure the preservation of one's natural interests is through military force. For over forty years of the twentieth century, the United States and the Soviet Union shadowed each other in the Arctic. Nuclear powered submarines maneuvered below the ice caps and long range bombers and fighters flew above them. However, when the Berlin Wall fell, so did the importance of this area for strategists and military planners.[42]

Climate change forced policy makers to return their attention to the situation above the Arctic Circle and they in turn directed the Defense Department to adjust their guidance to the uniformed services. The result of this reassessment was the 2010 Quadrennial Defense Review's acknowledgement that melting ice in the Arctic increases direct threats to the United States.[43] The subsequent delegation of responsibility for the Arctic to NORTHCOM operationalized American military policy. Not only were Combatant Command boundaries adjusted, but other visible signals of the importance of the Arctic are noticeable. NORTHCOM leaders expanded their relationship with the Canadian Defense Forces and continue to develop closer military to military relationships with Norway, and Denmark, and even Russia.

While the Army, Air Force, and Marines undoubtedly need to increase their cold weather capabilities as well as their winter related training, the missions of the United States Navy and Coast Guard must expand significantly as the Arctic requires more attention. New operating areas for surface ships and Coast Guard cutters, increased maritime security operations, and most importantly ensuring freedom of navigation and the right of free passage require additional planning, training, and proper equipment.[44] Today, the Coast Guard has only three icebreakers capable of operating effectively in the Arctic. Additionally, the harsh environment requires modifications to current training and support equipment. Fuel storage, maintenance procedures, and housing to operate in the High North have not been thought through or considered in planning or budgets. As the Chief of Naval Operations, Admiral Gary Roughead said, "I really believe now is the time to start thinking about that..."[45]

In order to address the shortfalls, increase maritime awareness, and reduce overall costs Defense Department officials started to collaborate with other countries in the Arctic. United States and Canadian military exercises have been conducted in the region, intelligence personnel work together on Arctic assessments, and discussions are underway for joint investment and technology development.[46] In the future, the United States must also increase its diplomatic involvement in the Arctic. Finally realizing that they failed to focus on this important area for the last 20 years is a start, but the diplomatic gap remains quite large and any hesitancy to embrace cooperative and multilateral efforts reflects poorly on the future of the Arctic Council and other international institutions.

Recommendations

The potential of the Arctic to increase the quality of life for all nations on Earth requires those with a direct interest in the region to work together on solutions now. The climate and geography are extreme. The utility of force in the area is costly and challenging. The post modern international system requires that Arctic nations address these issues with a different kind of strategy. In particular, the United States, if it desires to remain a world leader must modify its policies and implement several recommendations to ensure their vital interests are addressed.

First, the Obama Administration and the United States Senate must make ratification of the United Nations Convention on the Law of the Sea (UNCLOS) its top priority. Failure to acknowledge international law with regard to making territorial claims in the Arctic not only limits the area available for resource exploration, but illustrates the United States' unwillingness to be a partner in the international community and supporter of regional alliances. UNCLOS provides legal certainty by allowing the United States to submit claims to an extended continental shelf which guarantees access and rights to additional Arctic territory.[47] Additionally, America's support for the United Nations and the Arctic Council builds prestige in those institutions and expands American leadership opportunities and influence.

Second, the United States must embrace diplomacy and international cooperation not out of fear, but out of confidence and strength. Sharing the resources of the Arctic, showing deference to the other Arctic nations, and participating in joint exercises with smaller nations not only increases the wealth and readiness of America, but serves its interests by improving how it is viewed by the rest of the world.[48] Those responsible for the strategic policy of the United States must recognize and accept that the best way to secure its vital interests in the Arctic is through collective security and cooperation with other Arctic nations. While Americans rarely utilize this type of policy, this kind of arrangement is necessary for both economic and operational reasons. The cost of deploying, employing, and equipping military forces as well as locating and extracting resources in the Arctic precludes individual nations from acting independently. As Sir Rupert Smith identified in *The Utility of Force*, multinational operations will be normative in the future and "structural change is particularly important."[49]

The Arctic Council provides an opportunity to develop fully an entity whose sole purpose is to manage and direct joint operations in a peaceful and relatively low threat environment. It is a system where the endstate for the region is predetermined and agreed upon prior to the commencement of any operations. All parties in this arrangement share the risk equally and with each successful venture divide up the economic and political benefits.

Collaboration and cooperation of this type will not come easy or fast. But if discussions start now, most of the issues can be addressed and solutions put into place before the ice melts in 2030. Diplomatically, the Obama Administration must take the lead in the Arctic Council as well as preserve its relationship with other key members of the world community. Russia is a major player in the Arctic and the United States must improve its relationship with Moscow to ensure success in the region. Because Russia is so dependent on the High North for its international standing, brinksmanship is not the best way to engage them. Technological sharing agreements, infrastructure development, and improving environmental protection may be better methods of gaining Russia's trust, confidence, and cooperation.

China does not have any direct claim to the Arctic, but it has a tremendous amount to gain from transit routes and high end resources. As the world's largest growing economy, the ability of the Chinese to negotiate the best price for materials that it imports and exports is vital to its national interest. Free access to the Northwest and Northeast Passage brings new and required materials and it allows quicker and cheaper movement of goods to market. American participation and leadership in the Arctic Council prevents China from gaining an unfair advantage and guarantees equality, access, and security for all nations. Therefore, the United States has a strategic responsibility to become and remain deeply involved in the region.

On the military front, several nations already conduct joint training and exercises to build a better team and to share costs. Expansion of these types of ventures to all members of the Arctic Council and the procurement of interoperable equipment is necessary for the successful operation of any regional alliance. Common operating procedures and standardized tactics improve coordination and increase unity of effort. The savings in research, development, and fielding of new systems and equipment alone are critical in tough economic times.

Third, the United States must ensure that its own internal structures are organized and prepared for their responsibilities in the Arctic. Delegating authority for the Arctic to NORTHCOM is only part of the solution. A successful Arctic policy requires a whole of government approach. The 2011 change to the Unified Command Plan is a start and at least provides unity of command for the region. However, without unity of effort success will not be accomplished. The Department of Homeland Security, Department of State, Department of the Interior, and the Department of Transportation all have a role to play in the implementation of the Arctic Policy of the United States. Only through an effective interagency process and proper direction from the National Security Council will Arctic planning, budgeting, and execution be synchronized and effective.

Success for America in the Arctic requires strategic leaders to balance both hard and soft power. The challenge is modifying its behavior after exhibiting a hegemonic personality for the last six decades. The best way to achieve the interests of the United States in the Arctic involves consultation, cooperation, and the acceptance of other nations' ideas. The United States can no longer make decisions and dictate how the world will act; it must learn to guide others toward mutually accepted positions.

Ultimately, the future implementation of any United States Arctic Policy competes with other important domestic and foreign policy interests. While climate change in the Arctic is ongoing, the speed and depth of its impact fluctuates over time as does its importance to the American people. Therefore, the way the United States will carry out its policy in the High North remains uncertain. As a post modern state, the opportunity to engage collectively and through cooperation with international and regional organizations makes the most sense economically and politically. The challenge is to operationalize this way of thinking. It requires a willingness to accept less than optimal results in return for lower costs, shared responsibility, and transparent actions. In the end, achieving the best solution for the Arctic requires the United States to reassess

and rethink both its use of diplomacy and military force.

Endnotes

[1] "Iced-in Nome, Alaska Gets Oil," January 16, 2012, http://www.disasternews.net/news/article.php?articleid=4395 (accessed January 31, 2012).

[2] Lawson W. Bingham, "Think Again: The Arctic," *Foreign Policy*, (Sep/Oct 2010): 2.

[3] Ronald O'Rourke, *Changes in the Arctic: Background and Issues for Congress* (Washington, DC: U.S. Library of Congress, Congressional Research Service, April 2011), 8.

[4] Heather A.Conley and Jamie Kraut, "US Strategic Interests in the Arctic: An Assessment of Current Challenges and New Opportunities for Cooperation," *Center for Strategic and International Studies* (April 2010): 6.

[5] Ibid., 2.

[6] Bingham, "Think Again: The Arctic," 4.

[7] Ibid., 6.

[8] Ibid., 7.

[9] Ibid., 8.

[10] Ibid., 6.

[11] Ibid., 12.

[12] Ibid., 21.

[13] Ibid., 22.

[14] Rupert Smith, *The Utility of Force: The Art of War in the Modern World* (New York: Vintage Books, 2008), 25-26.

[15] Ibid., 347.

[16] Robert F. Cooper, *The Post-Modern State and the World Order* (London: The Foreign Policy Center, Demos, 2000), 15.

[17] Ibid., 43.

[18] Ibid.

[19] Ibid., 17.

[20] Conley and Kraut, "US Strategic Interests in the Arctic," 24.

[21] O'Rourke, "Changes in the Arctic," 14.

[22] Geoffrey Till, *Seapower: A Guide for the 21st Century* (United Kingdom: Routledge, 2009), 247.

[23] Cooper, "The Post Modern State," 20.

[24] Randy Boswell, "Canada Asserts Arctic Policy, Sovereignty." *National Post (Ontario)*, July 26, 2010.

[25] Jeffrey Jones, "Canadian Arctic Gas Pipeline Faces Further Delay," *Reuters*, March 15, 2010.

[26] Conley and Kraut, "US Strategic Interests in the Arctic," 17.

[27] Stephen J. Harper, *Canada First Defence Strategy* (Ottawa: National Defence and Canadian Forces, May 2008), 8.

[28] Ibid.,17.

[29] Conley and Kraut, "US Strategic Interests in the Arctic," 19.

[30] Nikolaj Peterson, "The Arctic as a New Arena for Danish Foreign Policy: The Ilulissat Initiative and its Implications," in Danish Foreign Policy Yearbook 2009, ed. Hanna Huidt and Hans Mouritzen (Copenhagen: Danish Institute for International Studies, 2009), 55.

[31] Danish Ministry of Defence, *Danish Defence Agreement 2010-2014* (Copenhagen, Danish Ministry of Defence June 24, 2009), 12.

[32] Paul Sigurd Hilde, "Norway and the Arctic: The End of Dreams," Atlantic Community, March 11, 2010, http://www.atlantic-community.org/index/articles/view/Norway_and_the_Arctic:_The_End_of_Dreams%3F (accessed January 31, 2012).

[33] Norwegian Ministry of Foreign Affairs, *The Norwegian Government's High North Strategy* (Oslo, Norwegian Ministry of Foreign Affairs, December 2006), 17.

[34] BarentsObserver.com, "Norwegian Army Moves North," August 5, 2009, http://barentsobserver.com/norwegian-army-moves-north.4616549.html (accessed January 31, 2012)

[35] Conley and Kraut, "US Strategic Interests in the Arctic," 24.

[36] Conley and Kraut, "US Strategic Interests in the Arctic," 25.

[37] Conley and Kraut, "US Strategic Interests in the Arctic," 24.

[38] O'Rourke, "Changes in the Arctic," 6.

[39] George W. Bush, *National Security Presidential Directive/NSPD 66 and Homeland Security Presidential Directive/HSPD 25*, January 9, 2009, Section III, A (1).

[40] Ibid., Section III, A (4).

[41] Will Rogers, "To Secure U.S. Interests in the Arctic, Ratifying UNCLOS is Key," May 17, 2011, http://www.cnas.org/blogs/naturalsecurity/2011/05/secure-us-interests-arctic-ratifying-unclos-key.html (accessed January 31, 2012.

[42] O'Rourke, "Changes in the Arctic," 37.

[43] Robert M. Gates, *Quadrennial Defense Review* (Washington, DC: U.S. Department of Defense, February 2010), 19.

[44] Bush, *NSPD 66*, Section III, B.

[45] Lance M. Bacon, "Icebreaker," *Armed Forces Journal*, (March 2010): 16-19.

[46] Christopher J. Castelli, "American, Canadian Defense Officials Tighten Ties on Arctic Bases," *Inside the Navy*, May 3, 2010.

[47] Herbert Carmen, Christine Parthemore, and Will Rogers, "Broadening Horizons: Climate Change and the US Armed Forces," Center for a New American Security (April 2010): 10.

[48] Fareed Zakaria, *The Post-American World* (New York: W.W. Norton and Company, 2009), 229-230.

[49] Smith, *The Utility of Force,* 398.